Is It Important to Buy

AMERICAN GOODS?

By Donna Reynolds

Published in 2021 by
KidHaven Publishing, an Imprint of Greenhaven Publishing, LLC
353 3rd Avenue
Suite 255
New York, NY 10010

Designer: Deanna Paternostro
Editor: Jennifer Lombardo

Photo credits: Cover Ty Wright/Bloomberg via Getty Images; p. 5 (top left) Anton Gvozdikov/Shutterstock.com; p. 5 (top right) Novikov Aleksey/Shutterstock.com; p. 5 (bottom) kakteen/Shutterstock.com; p. 7 Jonathan Weiss/Shutterstock.com; p. 9 Kzenon/Shutterstock.com; p. 11 (top) Jenson/Shutterstock.com; p. 11 (bottom) PopTika/Shutterstock.com; p. 13 Marcin Krzyzak/Shutterstock.com; p. 15 (main) ranplett/E+/Getty Images; p. 15 (inset) John Carey/Photolibrary/Getty Images Plus/Getty Images; p. 17 (main) AYA images/Shutterstock.com; p. 17 (inset) Sharaf Maksumov/Shutterstock.com; p. 19 Tyler Olson/Shutterstock.com; p. 21 (notepad) ESB Professional/Shutterstock.com; p. 21 (markers) Kucher Serhii/Shutterstock.com; p. 21 (photo frame) FARBAI/iStock/Thinkstock; p. 21 (inset, left) Art Konovalov/Shutterstock.com; p. 21 (inset, middle-left) micro10x/Shutterstock.com; p. 21 (inset, middle-right) Michael Traitov/Shutterstock.com; p. 21 (inset, right) StevenK/Shutterstock.com.

Library of Congress Cataloging-in-Publication Data

Names: Reynolds, Donna, author.
Title: Is it important to buy American goods? / Donna Reynolds.
Description: New York : KidHaven Publishing, [2021] | Series: Points of
  view | Includes bibliographical references and index.
Identifiers: LCCN 2019052394 (print) | LCCN 2019052395 (ebook) | ISBN
  9781534534346 (library binding) | ISBN 9781534534322 (paperback) | ISBN
  9781534534353 (ebook) | ISBN 9781534534339 (set)
Subjects: LCSH: Consumption (Economics)–United States–Juvenile
  literature. | Imports–United States–Juvenile literature. | Consumer
  behavior–United States–Juvenile literature. | United
  States–Commerce–Juvenile literature.
Classification: LCC HC110.C6 R49 2021 (print) | LCC HC110.C6 (ebook) |
  DDC 339.4/70973–dc23
LC record available at https://lccn.loc.gov/2019052394
LC ebook record available at https://lccn.loc.gov/2019052395

Printed in the United States of America

Some of the images in this book illustrate individuals who are models. The depictions do not imply actual situations or events.

CPSIA compliance information: Batch #BS20K: For further information contact Greenhaven Publishing LLC, New York, New York at 1-844-317-7404.

Please visit our website, www.greenhavenpublishing.com. For a free color catalog of all our high-quality books, call toll free 1-844-317-7404 or fax 1-844-317-7405.

Find us on

CONTENTS

SIDES

Many **items** will say where they were made. Sometimes there's a tag or sticker on it. Other times, it's printed right on the item. How often do you look to see where things were made before you buy them?

Some Americans think it's important to buy goods that were made in the United States. Others care less about where goods are made. These people generally don't think it's bad to buy American goods, but they also don't think it's something all Americans must do. Understanding both opinions is an important part of making up your own mind about the things you buy.

Know the Facts!

Something that's bought in the country where it was made is called a domestic good. Goods that aren't domestic are exported, or sent, from the country where they were made and imported, or brought, into the country where they're sold.

Countries around the world have both imported and domestic goods for sale, but some have more of one than the other.

WORLD

In the past, most of a country's goods were domestic. Imported goods were generally too expensive for anyone except the richest people to afford. Today, imported goods are often cheaper than domestic goods in the United States.

Even if something is made in the United States, it's not unusual for some parts of it to be imported. For example, a dress might be sewn in the United States, but the **fabric** might be imported from another country. Some people think the most important thing is where the product is put together. Others think the fact that some parts of domestic goods are imported means it doesn't matter what kinds of goods they buy.

Know the Facts!

President Donald Trump put a tax on some imported items to make them more expensive for Americans to buy. He thought this would help American companies, but it hurt some of them.

Ford cars are made in America,
but some of their parts are imported.

Creating More
JOBS

When you buy something that was made in the United States, you're helping the American **economy**. The money you spend goes to an American business and American workers. If the business does well, it might be able to give more people jobs. Creating jobs helps people because it means the people who were hired will have more money to buy things for their families.

Many people think Americans should help their own economy and their own workers instead of other countries'. They generally want jobs to be created in the United States. If people buy a lot of imported goods, that creates jobs in other countries instead.

Know the Facts!

"Reshoring" means getting businesses that have moved to other countries to move back to the United States. One of the main goals of reshoring is to create more jobs for American workers.

Many Americans worry about not having jobs. Buying domestic goods creates jobs because businesses need to hire more workers so they can keep making enough of their product to meet **demands**.

Not the Only
PROBLEM

Many people don't think that buying imported goods is the only reason why jobs can be hard to find in the United States. They point out that many jobs have been lost because of automation, which is when a computer or robot does a job that a human—or, often, several humans—used to do.

Automation has helped companies make products faster and more cheaply, so they keep **replacing** human workers with machines. This is why many people don't think it's important to buy American goods. They know businesses might not actually hire more workers even if more people are buying their products. They might use more machines instead.

Know the Facts!

According to *Foreign Affairs* magazine, nearly 5 million American jobs have been lost to automation since 2000.

Today, machines do a lot of the work that humans used to do. They won't entirely take the place of people, though, because someone still needs to create and operate the machines.

FAIR

People who support buying American goods say the number of jobs that creates isn't the only important thing. They also care about how safe and fair those jobs are for workers.

The U.S. government makes rules about safety and how long someone can work at one time, but some other countries don't. In the factories in those countries, people often work very long hours for very little money. The factories are often dirty and dangerous, or unsafe. These kinds of factories are called sweatshops. Many Americans buy domestic products so they know their money isn't supporting a sweatshop in another country.

Know the Facts!

In China and India, some workers make only $2 per hour. This is because the factory owners want to keep all the **profits** for themselves instead of sharing the money with their workers.

In some other countries, people work in poor conditions because it's the only kind of work they can find. Many sweatshops make children work, which is against the law in the United States.

Being a Careful
CONSUMER

Some people point out that not all companies outside the United States treat their workers badly. They say it's important for consumers, or people who buy things, to do **research** about a company before they buy something from it. For many people, the way a company treats its workers is more important than where its products are made.

For example, almost all coffee sold in the United States is imported. Some people only buy coffee that has a "fair trade" label on it. Companies that make this coffee have promised to pay and treat their workers well and to make coffee in a way that doesn't hurt the **environment**.

Know the Facts!

Coffee isn't the only fair trade item. Other items you can find with the fair trade label include bananas, avocados, chocolate, tea, and ice cream.

Fair trade companies make a promise to take care of their workers. This makes many Americans feel better about buying some imported goods.

PLANET

Some people think the most important thing about buying domestic goods is taking care of the environment. Anything that's imported has to travel. This means trucks and planes are going back and forth, putting a lot of carbon dioxide into the air. This is a gas that traps heat. As the air gets warmer, the **climate** changes. Imported products aren't the only cause of climate change, but they're part of it.

People who are worried about the environment try to buy things that were made or grown as locally as possible. For example, they might buy food from a nearby farm instead of buying imported tomatoes at the grocery store.

Know the Facts!

"Food miles" is a term that's used to describe how far a certain food has been carried from where it was grown. People who want to help the environment generally try to look for foods with a low food mileage.

Some people choose to grow their own food instead of buying imported foods.

17

MONEY

Many people like the idea of buying American goods but care more about their **budget** than about where the product comes from. If a domestic item costs only a little more than an imported one, they might buy it. However, the bigger the difference between the prices gets, the less likely people are to buy the good that costs more—even if it was made in America.

When people don't have a lot of money, they don't feel like they have a choice about what kind of products to buy. They need to make sure they have food, clothing, housing, and other important things. If they pay too much for one thing, they'll have less money for the others.

Know the Facts!

In a 2016 **survey** of 1,076 adults, 67 percent said they would rather buy a cheaper imported product than a more expensive domestic product.

People are more
likely to buy
American goods
if they're the
cheapest option.

BOTH SIDES

Most people want to do what's best for their country's economy, for the world, and for their household. However, many people disagree about what "best" means. Some people think buying American goods is best. Others think it doesn't matter since the world is so connected today that at least part of their American-made goods often come from another country.

Now that you know both sides, what do you think? If you had $20 to spend, would you make sure you bought something that was made in the United States? Which arguments are you thinking about to help you make your choice?

Know the Facts!

More than half of all U.S. imports come from five countries: China, Canada, Mexico, Japan, and Germany.

Is it important to buy American goods?

YES

- It helps the American economy.

- The United States has rules to make sure the workers who make a product are treated well.

- Buying a domestic product is better for the environment.

- The most important thing about a product is where it was put together.

NO

- It's not the only thing that affects, or shapes, the economy.

- Some companies outside the United States treat their workers very well.

- Not everyone has enough money to buy domestic products if they're more expensive.

- Many American-made goods have parts from other countries.

There are many reasons why people think it's important to buy American goods. There are also many reasons why people think it isn't important at all. What do you think?

GLOSSARY

budget: A set amount of money or a plan for how to spend that money.

climate: The weather in an area over a long period of time.

demand: A strong request for something.

economy: The way in which goods and services are made, sold, and used in a country or area.

environment: The natural world around us.

fabric: Cloth.

item: A single thing.

profit: Money that is made.

replace: To take the place of.

research: Careful study that is done to find and report new knowledge about something.

survey: An activity in which many people are asked questions in order to gather facts about what most people think about something.

For More INFORMATION

WEBSITES

Ducksters: Economics
www.ducksters.com/money/economics.php
This website teaches the basics of economics, which is an important part of understanding the arguments for and against buying only American goods.

USA Love List
www.usalovelist.com
This website highlights products that are made in the United States.

BOOKS

Eagan, Rachel. *Trade in Our Global Community*. New York, NY: Crabtree Publishing Company, 2019.

Kenney, Karen Latchana, and Steve Stankiewicz. *Economics Through Infographics*. Minneapolis, MN: Lerner Publications, 2015.

Ogden, Charlie. *Fair Trade and Global Economy*. New York, NY: Crabtree Publishing Company, 2018.

INDEX